Warbler

Warbler

Poems by

Jane Schapiro

Cover design by Shay Culligan

Cover Art by Rita Blitt, *Fire Bird from the Music Celebrating Dorianna series,* 1999. Acrylic and oil on canvas, 50 x 60 in. Rita Blitt Legacy Collection, Mulvane Art Museum, Washburn University, Topeka, Kansas.

ISBN: 978-1-952326-23-3

Kelsay Books
502 South 1040 East, A-119
American Fork, Utah, 84003

Acknowledgments

I am grateful to the editors of the following journals where these poems originally appeared.

Ars-Medica: "My Cross-legged Monk"

Beltway Poetry Quarterly: "Cemetery"

Gargoyle: "Erosion," "Bashert"

The American Journal of Poetry: "Heartland"

The Awakenings Review: "Migraine," "Have You Ever"

The Cape Rock: "My Grandfather's Yearbook"

The Healing Muse: "Blessing for the Status Quo"

Prairie Schooner: "First Lesson in Faith"

The Sow's Ear: "Sanibel Island," "Gravity"

Contents

I

שִׁיר Shiri   13
Once Upon a Time   14
Fluency   15
Snow Globes   16
Diagnosis   17
Bashert   18
Visit to an Oracle   19
Blessing for the Status Quo   20
Prospect Hill Plantation Inn   21
Porcelain of Loss   22
Gravity   23
Cemetery   25
Lost Blog   26
We Will Win   27
Qi   28
Aria   29
Starling   31

II

My Cross-legged Monk   35

III

First Lesson in Faith   45
Grace   46
Sanibel Island   47
Absence   48
Erosion   49
Have You Ever   50
Heartland   51
Migraine   53
My Grandfather's High School Yearbook   55

I

In Memory of Shiri Rahamim
שירי רחמים
(1984–2015)
Tears are the soul bathing itself.

שִׁיר Shiri

(Translation: Song)

this song was jubilant
it was rock and roll
this song was understated
it was a lullaby
this song was proud
it was an anthem
this song was determined
it was a march
this song was lonely
it was an aria
this song was mystical
it was an incantation
this song was authentic
it was soul
this song was spontaneous
it was jazz
this song was grateful
it was a psalm
this song was emotional
it was the blues
this song was lyrical
it was a poem
this song was mournful
it was a dirge
this song was changing
it was a remix

this song is singing
it is memory

Once Upon a Time

there lived two sisters, Noa and Shiri. Shiri had cancer. She wanted
to journey from her home in Israel to see a Qi Master in China.
Noa agreed to accompany her. They boarded a plane then a bus
then a ferry. Shiri had marijuana drops to relieve her pain. She
rubbed them into her skin then tossed the bottle into her suitcase,
forgetting to throw the bottle away. She and Noa arrived at the pier
and waited in line at customs. As Shiri stepped forward to get her
passport stamped, search dogs started to bark. They circled. They
pulled. They lunged. The officers led Shiri to a room. Noa
watched. Should she go help? No that would attract attention. Noa
advanced through the line. She watched as Shiri took cosmetics out
of her purse, stalling: *This is blush that I put on my face, liner for
my eyes.* Noa finally arrives. *What's up? Anything wrong?* Shiri
was emptying her carry-on, leading the officers toward the pile.
The officers turned to sift through the items at which time Noa
switched her suitcase with Shiri's. The officers released them. And
they lived

...no...

the dogs

waiting

at the threshold.

Fluency

I called them peccadillos: little acts
I couldn't explain. Look how she peels her grapes,
will only drink tea in clear glass mugs.
In the beginning, that's all I had—
why does she keep a lamp on all night,
back her car into parking spots?
Without speech, habits protrude
like rocks in a dry riverbed.

Gradually she filled the space,
my dad, Sephardic, I was born in Holon.
Information trickled, flowed, then cascaded in.
Through nouns, verbs, anecdotes, tales,
a self emerged.

The grapes?
Her father used to skin the fruit,
lovingly slip them into her lunch.

The tea? Her Iranian roots:
Persians like to see their tea.

The car? An Israeli mindset:
be prepared—

which brings us to

the lamp

for terrors
we all understand.

Snow Globes

As she listed her rules—
one globe per site,
hometown doesn't count,
she had to have visited—
she'd pick up an orb and shake it.
Badlands, Paris, Grand Canyon.
Memories flittered, then stilled.
Ever been tempted to break one, I asked.
She laughed at the thought.
I didn't tell her I once smashed Disneyland,
watched it drain onto the ground.

Smiling, oblivious
to the cancer growing inside,
she reigned over her utopias.

Diagnosis

On a spring afternoon
as iridescent as this
the thought of you frozen
by a lit screen as the doctor
points to shaded spots,
is unbearable;
              nevertheless
I keep thinking of you.
I've read how at first
the world turns pale but later
there comes clarity, hues
intensify. This is my chance
to hear firsthand.
How does health look
from behind the barbed wire?

When we get together
I don't dare ask.

Bashert

Kizmet. Karma. Providence.
Every faith has one word
that quiets all the what if's and why's.
For Jews, *bashert* is the catch-all term,
the tarp we raise against the night.

Bashert, I came early/left late,
took the call/missed the call,
got the job/left the job, ran into him….
Bashert is the dot we place on our maps:
I am here, not there. It is meant to be.

But what about its antonym:
Anomaly, the doctor said
(cancer, stage 4, 28 years old).
No word can douse the heartache we feel
blazing like a hot coal inside.

Visit to an Oracle

Had you looked in her eyes
you would have seen
winds advancing
stirring dust.

Had you held her hand
you would have felt
a tremor, trees whipping
the salty air.

Had you tracked her movements
you would have noticed
birds dispersing,
flying low.

Had you listened
beyond words,
you would have heard
a warbler singing out fear.

Instead you offered her lemongrass tea.

Blessing for the Status Quo

Bless the state in which
we find ourselves
as we are.
Praise the *are,*
the in out in
of breath.
Behold the breath,
the you, the me,
the I.V. drip
drip drip drip
and fear.
Seek grace in the fear,
the state in which
we find ourselves here
as things are
as we are
inside this wreckage
now.

Prospect Hill Plantation Inn

Uncle Guy's House:
"This stately and handsome cottage is the oldest structure at Prospect Hill
constructed expressly for housing slaves."

Focusing on each floorboard
you tiptoed to the loft
where the fieldhands once slept.
Even with its hot tub and marble sink
your eyes fixed on the original plank.
Like a stenographer you noted each stir.
Every creak and groan snapped you awake.
Long before getting sick, you translated omens:
this butterfly, that fallen tree—
everywhere messages.
In the morning as we drove
to a yet another doctor,
you couldn't relax—
liberation? bondage?
as Prospect Hill's wooden sign
receded in the mirror.

Porcelain of Loss

Because
   you   died   in
   your   native
     tongue   a
                    language
incoherent to
me I
     entered
   grief   from
the
insideoutunshackled
   from
syntaxcondolences
                              shat
                    ter
                         ed
sounds
               skittered
                    across
the room

     what to say
                    what to
think

          among
                    mourners

          frac
               tured

Gravity

Mourning
is reserved
for parents
saying *Kaddish*
siblings
sitting shiva
peers
sharing stories
mentors
naming scholarships
employers
founding awards
neighbors
bringing meals
communities
hanging plaques

but for me who
was none of these
too old to be labeled friend
too needy to be a sage
title-less
yet
connected
for I also
crossed paths
with her life
was drawn into its eddy
that mighty whirl
feel it even now
while sitting
in a room
across the sea
for me

there is
no gesture
no blessing
no rite to perform
just a pull
tugging
deep inside
like an anchor
that won't dislodge
though I try
grab the word
grief: sharp sorrow
follow it down
See grieve gravare to burden
down
derivative of gravis heavy
and down
grave, gravity
to its source
the force by which a planet or other body
draws objects toward its center.

Cemetery

Jewish tradition holds that washing your hands when leaving the cemetery prevents the Angel of Death from following you.

Hard to believe a few drops
can keep death contained,
allow me to exit the valley of the shadow
without being trailed. In line at the spigot,
I wait my turn (just to be safe).
Who hasn't, at one time or another,
performed a rite (just to be safe).

When endangered we act to appease—
how many *hamsot* did we hang in your room: three? four?
each one bigger than the one before.
Red threads tied around wrists,
amulets hanging from necks…
What more could we do?
You even changed your name.
Together we would force
the evil eye to shift its gaze.

Yet, here we are.

After unlatching the gate,
I rinse my hands (just to be safe).

Lost Blog

Somewhere in the cloud
with your tooth-filled grin
your alias is lamenting men.
On the internet, keeping tabs,
she's recounting her love life,
the good dates, the bad.
Cradling a laptop and beer
on a Tel Aviv beach,
your pseudonym is typing
as high tide draws near.
She hasn't a clue you no longer exist
there will be no more names
to add to her list.

Anonymity is key, you claimed,
you never revealed her website or name.
I would love to find her,
set her straight—*no knight can win
against cold-hearted fate*—
but part of me still clings to hope,
would rather leave an encouraging post—
keep writing, dreaming—

We Will Win

Nothing—not the doctor's terminology,
your father's flood of tears,
your brother's ashen face,
your sister's dread-filled eyes,
not diagnosis, prognosis,
fear, shock—nothing—
nothing, nothing, nothing
could beat back the blazes of hope.

I remember your voice exploding,
igniting each word,
sending out sparks.
—*We Will Win*—
spread through, around
inside of me.

Though your promise burned to ash,
I return to that oath—its power,
its strength, its brilliant flame—
and shudder in its radiance.

Qi

When my year-old granddaughter dances
she moves her belly.
As the music plays,
she leans her stomach into each note.
I clap and laugh and
at some point,
I glimpse you,
sitting to the side, your fists
pressing your navel,
your voice explaining:
qi is here
look at children,
they move from here.
Then you vanish
except

the three of us
are now clapping
laughing
dancing
inside
melody
right
here.

Aria

Had
our plane landed on time
our bags arrived first
the roads been empty
your brother driven faster
the traffic lights stayed green
and yes had
you kept weaving
the air
one filament
at a time
wisp after
wisp
strand after
strand
like Penelope
stitching
unraveling
exhaling
inhaling
threading
your breath
in out
a few more
minutes
kept going
out in
a few
more…

From the back seat I hear
a cell phone,
voices,
Hebrew,
weeping,
your name,
rising,
filling my ears—

Shiri

your breathless chord
taking flight
up and out
of this compost
of sounds.

Starling

"Mozart discovered the starling in a Vienna pet shop, where the bird had somehow learned to sing the motif from his newest piano concerto. Enchanted, he bought the bird for a few kreuzer and kept it for three years before it died. Just how the starling learned Mozart's motif is a wonderful musico-ornithological mystery."
                    —From *Mozart's Starling* by Lyanda Lynn Haupt

I

In version one
the starling, perched
by an open window, hears Mozart
ambling the streets, whistling.
Drawn to the melody drifting in,
the bird begins to trill.

II

In version two,
Mozart, ambling the streets,
passes an open window, hears
the starling trilling.
Drawn to the melody drifting out,
he begins to transcribe.

31

III

"…there is one thing we know for certain: Mozart loved his starling." (Lyanda Lynn Haupt)

Trilled, whistled,
sung, or heard,
melody is the heroine: that pulsating
wave traversing space, connecting

bird and man,
as animate as an organism,
as invisible as air
as alive as memory.

IV

If I've learned anything
it's that the window must be open.

II

The Soul has Bandaged moments—
　　　　　　—Emily Dickinson

My Cross-legged Monk

"…you are more than your anxiety"
—A Mindfulness-Based Stress Reduction Workbook

with incense and flame
i look for you
my affable
logical
good-natured self
eyes closed
hands on lap
i search for
my buddha my imam
my cross-legged monk
are you near
am i warm
i am here
inhaling
exhaling
calling your name
teacher rabbi
master sage
lama rishi
guru seer
quiet
hush
namaste
peace
where are you
my yogi
where are you
my priest

*

Had I found my qi
in that kindergarten room
I might not have cried at my mother's goodbyes,
told my teacher that daily lie:
I bumped my head on the jungle gym.
If you, nirvana, had just appeared
I might have been spared—
(hold your breath when a siren goes by)
(close then reclose the closet door).
Each night I'd think of another decree,
add it like a hallowed stone
(make sure all pictures are hanging straight).
I was building a temple inside, an altar
where I could barter and plead—
let my parents be safe
(say *kayn aynhoreh* after every good thought)
safe safe
let us all be safe.

*

"In every calm and reasonable person there is a hidden second
person scared witless about death." Philip Roth

*

In this dimly lit waiting room
we sit wearing sunglasses filling out forms.
No music, no books, no words exchanged.
Bent over clipboards, we rank our pain:

How severe? How frequent? How long does each last?
One by one, the nurse calls our names,
takes our weight, blood pressure,
points to a room.
Oh Doctor, Neurologist, Headache Oz
Help ease our relentless throbs.

*

Will I be okay?

*

"Everybody wants peace, peace of mind
 Everybody needs peace, peace of mind
 All we need is some peace" Loggins & Messina

*

I shouldn't have taken this garden plot,
I have no idea how to reap or sow.
I wanted reprieve but hear only snarls,
worm-eaten tomatoes hissing.
Even my sunflowers betray,
hang their heads in the afternoon light.
Charred and blistered, their mammoth eyes
shadow me like sockets of night.
Dry-mouth, nauseous,
tangled in a mesh of unease,
I flail like the chipmunk stuck in my fence.
All the while a hawk circles and scolds:

intruder imposter predator prey.

*

Will I be okay?

*

"The way to stop worrying about death is to watch a lot of television." Don DeLillo

*

Seems everyone has an elixir
to help lure my appetite back.
Milkshakes, smoothies, warm pecan pie.
Like witches they offer magical brews:
chia seeds in dumplings and broth.
Each day I down a glass of Boost
as thoughts of food turn into dry heaves.
Look closely friends, you see me now
yet I am vanishing before your eyes.

*

Will Lexapro work?
Doctor: *It works for my family.*
Husband: *It's like gefilte fish for Jews.*

Mouth opens—
emits a laugh.

*

Google history:
how long does lexapro take to act
how long before lexapro takes effect
how long before lexapro kicks in
how much lexapro can one take
how quickly can lexapro work

*

Knit 1
Purl 2
Knit 1
Purl 2
Knit 1
"…the repetitive action of needlework can induce a relaxed state."
Dr. Herbert Benson

*

Will I be okay?

*

Breathe in
I know I'm breathing in.
Breathe out
I know I'm breathing out.

*

"Peace is not a thought, not a concept, it is a nonverbal
experience." Bhante Henepola Gunaratana

and anguish is not
a metaphor
not an altar or garden
or socket of night
not a worm-eaten tomato
or hawk in flight
not a chipmunk
or blistered eye
not a charred sunflower
or jungle gym lie
it is not incense
or flame
it doesn't reside
in a waiting room
it is not nausea dry heaves
a throbbing migraine
not narrative
with beginning and end

not dialogue plot
theme or lesson
it is not fact or fiction
true or false
not rhyme myth
snarl or hiss
not...

*

ommmmmmmmmmm
mmmmmmmmmmm
mmmmmmmmmm
mmmmmmmmm
mmmmmmmm
mmmmmmm
mmmmmm
mmmmm
mmmm
mmm
mm
m

*

You
will
be
okay

*

Was it time or trust
that opened a vein,
ushered in warm, merciful,
honey-soaked sleep?

With venetian blinds
half-drawn I awoke in a
sun-streaked room

*

hungry

III

Out of the mocking-bird's throat, the musical shuttle
—Walt Whitman

First Lesson in Faith

Even the blank spaces
are God given, the rabbi explained
while unrolling the scroll. Focus
on a letter and you'll find
beneath the black ink, another one
etched in white.

Leaning forward, I squinted one eye,
then the other. Keep looking,
he urged, his pointer
circling the parchment. We lingered
like two figures in an unlit field, he,
with his outstretched arm, insisting,

and I, scanning the heavens.
Yes, there it is,
I finally declared,
as I used to while waiting
for Orion's belt to emerge
from three lonely stars.

Grace

After the receptionist calls your name and
you follow her through the heavy beige door, after
you enter the dressing room, slip off
your clothes, waist up, join the circle
of gowned women who keep pulling closed
their paper drapes, after
picking up *People,* reading news of
J. Lo then following the technician into a room
where she loads, squeezes, flattens
your breasts between glass plates,
lean forward, hold your breath, after
returning to your seat, picking up the same magazine but
this time just staring at the same few
words, wanting to stay in that safe in-between
like Schrödinger's cat, after sitting
there, hoping, praying to be called, no
Please God let me not be called, after
waiting, waiting, finally,
a name, your name, and then,
three words, hear them? yes,
those three
merciful, lucky, spondaic words,
you can go.

Sanibel Island

Between her and help the causeway spans.
I can't stand to see him grow old.
She piles one worry on top of the next like sandbags:
He's shuffling, forgetful, seems fatigued.
From the shore she watches for clouds,
panics at the slightest wind.
If only he would agree to pack up, move
to the mainland with their friends.
Instead he clings to luck. *What if*
he falls, has a stroke, a heart attack?
Lanes arch across the gulf. On a clear day,
she can just make out the hospital.
If she weren't so worried, she'd laugh at this
old woman's pot of gold. But the road
is a bleached rainbow, its concrete a covenant:
From here there is only one way off.

Absence

"To explain their observations, scientists say, they must answer a
question that sounds paradoxical: How much does emptiness
weigh?" *News Item*

She offers her husband's last days,
how he grew heavier with each lost pound.
Ever since he disappeared, she can feel his absence

pressing against her like a headwind, pushing
her back and back.
Her life contracts around

single tasks that once floated
invisibly through her days: folding clothes,
sweeping floors, making soup in the microwave—

each act's an orbit drawing her in.
Even the squares of Sunday crosswords
have taken on weight, collapsed

in their white holes. Sometimes, in the mirror,
she'll spot her former self like a star,
reflecting a fire long since burned out.

Erosion

happens so slowly
      you don't notice
you're dozing
      earlier each night,
settling deeper
      into your chair.
Between now
      and your youth
a canyon
      has formed. From
above you
      see only tiers
switchbacks
      curving. Too tired
to hike
      (your knees the heat)
you scan postcards
      look for freshwater.

Have You Ever

felt the urge to jump?
On our walk, we traded answers:
tenth floor of a Baltimore hotel,
Grand Canyon's northern rim.
Once we started we couldn't stop.

Have you ever screamed in a theatre,
or held your arm
so it wouldn't swipe china off
a department store shelf? Like girls
in a game of Go Fish, we sorted
and matched. How about stealing?

Have you ever grabbed a blouse,
headed toward an exit or
been tempted while driving
to head the wrong way,
leave your kids behind?
Queen of Spades,

Queen of Hearts,
we draw them both,
like that wife on the cruise
who leapt over the rail
then grabbed the rope
fastened onto the deck.

Heartland

Leaning over the kitchen sink
she turns up the radio. A witness
is telling his account.

I was lying in bed when I felt my room shake...

With a knife she slits the plastic bag, yanks
a half-frozen chicken out.

At first I thought a gas line had burst, but then I heard another
blast, and another...

She turns on the faucet, sprays hot water
over the breast.

From my front lawn I saw smoke...

With a quick jab she thrusts
her fist inside, tries to grab
the giblets and neck.
Sometimes the bag of organs tears.
She knows she should be patient—slowly
work the innards out.

After the third blast it was silent.

Clots of red ice circle
the drain. She looks
at the clock. Any minute
kids will be home,
the dog will bark,
lemonade will stick to the floor.
Telephone, screams, canned
laughter from the living room.

An expert is being interviewed.

Domestic terrorism can be the most frightening.

The screen door slams.

Migraine

"What do we know beyond the rapture and the dread?"
—Stanley Kunitz

I.

Pain, please I beg of you.
Let me sleep, let darkness rock me out of this world.
Take what you like, just go away.

What am I supposed to learn, what tidbit of truth
might I find circling this toilet bowl?
Please Pain, I beg of you.

Beyond the threshold, children's voices:
Can we come in? What should we eat? Everyone,
can you go away?

Outside my room, questions pound
against my door. Do not disturb,
I beg of you.

How readily I betray,
pray to that Golden Calf:
Pain, take what you like.

Would I bind my first-born,
lead her to the altar?
Pain, please, I beg of you,
take what you like just go away.

II.

There must be a blessing for when the veil lifts,
reveals the world as a luminous bride,
a few words we can whisper upon our return
when we kneel and kiss the Promised Land.
Anchored to the morning light, I sit,
mug of coffee, smell of toast,
the dog sleeping against my feet.
Ah, sweet life. Sweet, inviting life.

III

Down the street,
azaleas have bloomed.
A yard has exploded
in pinks and reds.
Neighbors gather.
Magnificent. Divine.
Nobody mentions the tangle of shrubs
that spawned such a glorious sight.

My Grandfather's High School Yearbook

All day I've been studying these faces,
hunched like a jeweler over his stones.
The eyes hold the answers.
I chisel at blank stares,
try to break into their depths,
but in eyes which never blink,
there are only frozen ponds,
silent, dark.

Perhaps the lips will tell;
the way they come together,
drift apart,
wrinkle at the corners.
These lines are the threads
that bind their seams.
I tug but each face remains fixed
like a snag on a sweater sleeve.

In the last row, second from the right,
a girl looks out, her arm draped
around the shoulder of her classmate.
It is these which reveal us;
an arm around a shoulder,
a hand inside another,
the crossings we make
before moving on.

About the Author

Jane Schapiro is the author of two volumes of poetry, *Tapping This Stone* (Washington Writers' Publishing House Award, 1995) and *Let The Wind Push Us Across* (Antrim House, 2017) a photographic and poetry narrative of her 1976 bicycle trip across the U.S. Her nonfiction book *Inside a Class Action: The Holocaust and the Swiss Banks* (University of Wisconsin, 2003) was selected for the Notable Trials Library. Her chapbook, *Mrs. Cave's House,* won the 2012 Sow's Ear Poetry Chapbook competition. Her poems have appeared in *The American Scholar, Prairie Schooner, The Gettysburg Review, The Southern Review, The Women's Review of Books, Yankee,* among others. She is a mother of three daughters and lives with her husband in Fairfax, VA.

Visit Jane's website at www.janeschapiro.com